CUTE & EASY · *Easter* · CAKE

Cute & Easy Easter Cake Toppers!

Contributors

Following a career in finance, Amanda Mumbray launched her cake business in 2010 and has gone from strength to strength, delighting customers with her unique bespoke creations and winning several Gold medals at various International Cake Shows. Amanda's **Clever Little Cupcake** company is based near Manchester, UK: www.cleverlittlecupcake.co.uk

Amanda Mumbray

Angela Morrison grew up in Venezuela around a wide variety of food and desserts, but it was when she moved to Virginia Beach, Va that her business **'Cakes by Angela Morrison'** was born. She has a wide online following for her super cute cake topper creations and her work has been published in many cake magazines and blogs.

Angela Morrison

Lesley Grainger has been imaginative since birth and has baked since she was old enough to hold a spatula. When life-saving surgery prompted a radical rethink, Lesley left a successful corporate career to pursue her passion for cake making. Lesley is based in Greenock, Scotland. Say 'hello' at: www.lesleybakescakes.co.uk

Lesley Grainger

Naomi from Calgary, Alberta-based **'Tea Party Cakes'** found her passion for cake decorating in 2010 when she took a course at a local craft store, and her work has since been featured in a host of cake magazines and websites. Naomi is also a regular contributor to *SugarEd Productions Online School*.

Naomi Hubert

First published in 2015 by Kyle Craig Publishing

Text and illustration copyright © 2015 Kyle Craig Publishing

Editor: Alison McNicol

Design: Julie Anson

ISBN: 978-1-908-707-61-1

A CIP record for this book is available from the British Library.

A Kyle Craig Publication

www.kyle-craig.com

Contents

Welcome!

Welcome to 'Easter!', the latest title in the **Cute & Easy Cake Toppers Collection**.

Each book in the series focuses on a specific theme, and here we have compiled a gorgeous selection of beautiful cake toppers that are perfect for any Easter celebration!

Whether you're an absolute beginner or an accomplished cake decorator, these projects are suitable for all skill levels, and we're sure that you will have as much fun making them as we did!

Enjoy!

Fondant/Sugarpaste/Gumpaste

Fondant/Sugarpaste – Ready-made fondant, also called ready to roll icing, is widely available in a selection of fantastic colours. Most regular cake decorators find it cheaper to buy a larger quantity in white and mix their own colours using colouring pastes or gels. Fondant is used to cover entire cakes, and as a base to make modelling paste for modelling and figures (see below).

Modelling Paste – Used throughout this book. Firm but pliable and dries faster and harder than fondant/sugarpaste. When making models, fondant can be too soft so we add CMC/Tylose powder to thicken it.

Gumpaste – Also known as 'Florist Paste'. More pliable than fondant, but dries very quickly and becomes quite hard, so it is widely used for items like flowers that are delicate but need to hold their shape when dry. Gumpaste can be made by adding Gum-Tex/Gum Tragacanth to regular fondant.

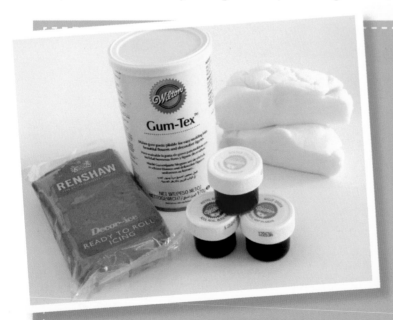

How to Make Modelling Paste

Throughout this book we refer to 'paste', meaning modelling paste. You can convert regular shop-bought fondant into modelling paste by adding CMC/Tylose powder, which is a thickening agent.

Add approx 1 tsp of CMC/Tylose powder to 225g (8oz) of fondant/sugarpaste. Knead well and leave in an airtight freezer bag for a couple of hours.

Add too much and it will crack. If this happens, add in a little shortening (white vegetable fat) to make it pliable again.

Tools

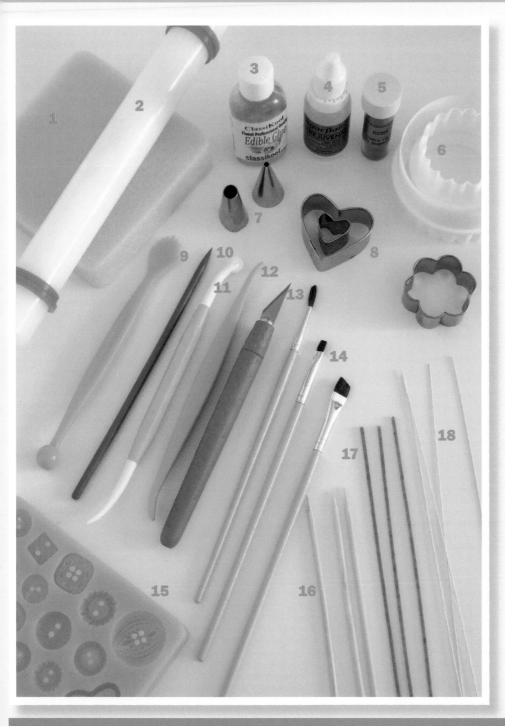

1 Foam Pad – holds pieces in place while drying.

2 Rolling pin – acrylic works better than wooden when working with fondant/paste.

3 Edible glue – essential when creating models. See below.

4 Rejuvenator spirit – mix with food colourings to create an edible paint.

5 Petal Dust, pink – for adding a 'blush' effect to cheeks.

6 Round and scalloped cutters – a modelling essential.

7 Piping nozzles – used to shape mouths and indents.

8 Shaped cutters – various uses.

9 Ball tool/serrated tool – another modelling essential.

10 Small pointed tool – used to create details like nostrils and holes.

11 Quilting tool – creates a stitched effect.

12 Veining tool – for adding details to flowers and models.

13 Craft knife/scalpel – everyday essential.

14 Brushes – to add finer details to faces.

15 Moulds – create detailed paste buttons, fairy wings and lots more.

16 Wooden skewers – to support larger models.

17 Spaghetti strands – also used for support.

18 Coated craft wire – often used in flower making.

Edible Glue

Whenever we refer to 'glue' in this book, we of course mean 'edible glue'. You can buy bottles of edible glue, which is strong and great for holding larger models together. You can also use a light brushing of water, some royal icing, or make your own edible glue by dissolving ¼ teaspoon tylose powder in 2 tablespoons warm water. Leave until dissolved and stir until smooth. This will keep for up to a week in the refrigerator.

Making Faces

The animal faces featured in this book vary in terms of detail and difficulty. If you're a complete beginner, you may opt to use simple shapes and edible pens to draw on simple features. As your confidence grows, you can use fondant for eyes and pupils, edible paint for features, or combine these methods for some great detailing.

Sugar pearls or balls of fondant can be used for eyes.

A mixture of fondant, pen and petal dust creates a cute face.

Contrasting paste creates a cute muzzle.

Pink petal dust adds blush to cheeks.

Edible pens can be used to draw on simple features.

Black fondant with white fondant or non-pareils make detailed eyes.

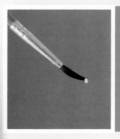

When adding tiny pieces of fondant for eyes, use a moist fine brush.

Cupcake Toppers

When making small figures for cupcakes, it's great to place each on a topper disc, and place this on top of a lovely swirl of buttercream. This way the figure can be removed and kept, and the child can tuck into the main cupcake.

Regular round cutters are essentials, and there are also a great selection of embossing tools and sheets out there that, when pressed into your rolled paste, will create cool quilting effects on your disc. Make your discs first and allow them to harden before you fix your figures to them.

Some figures may use a toothpick or skewer for support, so be sure to take care with these around small children.

You can also combine a scalloped cutter with the point of a small, round piping nozzle to create discs with cut-out holes.

Plunger cutters are a great way to add cute details to your models. They cut and then 'push' each small piece out, making it easy to cut small flowers, leaves and shapes.

Painting Details

Many of the projects in this book have beautiful details painted onto the mini items. Mixing regular gel or paste food colouring, or lustre dusts, with rejuvenator spirit will create edible paint in any colour you need. Keep a small collection of fine paintbrushes handy too!

Coloured details – mix your regular food colouring with rejuvenator spirit to create edible paint.

White paint – Americolor Bright White gel paste colour is strong enough to paint on clear white details.

Materials

Modelling paste:
Pale pink
Dark Pink
Lemon
Pale green
Pale blue
White
Brown
Edible pen/paint: black
Edible glue
Lustre dust: pink
Rice Krispie bars

Tools

Craft knife / scalpel
Veining tool
Quilting wheel
Fine paintbrush
Blossom cutter
FMM Frill cutter
Toothpicks

1 Stack three bars of rice krispies on top of each other to make the cottage.

2 Cut panels of thick paste to fit the 4 sides.

3 Make sure the joins cover all the rice krispies.

4 Completely cover all the sides, leaving the top exposed.

5 Cut two rectangular pieces and two triangles, for the roof, and set aside to dry completely.

6 Once dried, assemble the pieces to make a roof. Support these while the edible glue dries.

7 Cut a little arch shape for the door.

8 Cut two squares for the windows. Use edible glue to secure them.

9 Cut little strips for the window frames, angling the corners so they sit flush.

10 Cut very thin strips to make the window panes.

11 Add a little heart to the door, and a flattened ball of paste for the door handle.

12 Cut two frills, and attach one to the base of the roof, slightly over hanging the edge, and the other to cover the join at the roof apex.

13 Make a square out of some paste, and cut away a little V shape at the bottom.

14 Attach the chimney to the cottage, and attach a little ball of paste on top.

15 Paint on some details - wavy lines for the roof tiles, and polka dots to the front of the cottage.

16 Roll two tapered cones, and flatten at both ends.

17 Cut thin strips and attach to the top of the pots.

18 Roll out a cone of paste.

19 Use a veining tool to mark a spiral around the cone.

20 Attach it to the pot, and prick it with a toothpick all over.

21 Add a flattened ball of paste to the other pot.

22 Flatten a few teardrop shapes, and mark down the centre with a veining tool. Attach each 'leaf' to the side of the ball.

23 Cover the ball with lots of little blossoms.

24 For the bunny lady, roll out a teardrop shape, elongating the top half to make her body. Insert a toothpick.

25 Cut out a teardrop shape for her apron, and prick around the edges with a toothpick.

26 Cut a thin strip, and run the stitching wheel along both edges.

27 Attach a large ball for the head, and make two holes with the end of a paintbrush for the ears.

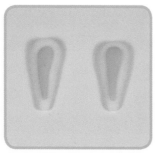

28 Roll teardrop shapes for the ears, and flatten. Roll smaller ones in pink, flatten and attach to the white ears.

29 Insert the ears in to the holes, and add a little ball of pink paste for the nose.

30 Roll two small balls for the sleeves, and make a hole with the end of paintbrush. Add teardrop shapes for the arms.

31 Attach the arms, and glue and position in place.

32 Paint or draw on the facial details, and dust the cheeks with a little petal dust.

33 Roll out a teardrop shape for the boy bunny, and mark a line up the middle with a veining tool. Insert a tooth-pick.

34 Add a little ball of white for the body.

35 Cut a thin strip for his belt, stitching both edges with a quilting wheel.

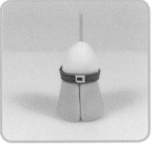

36 Cut out a little square, and then cut round that square to make the buckle.

37 Add a large ball for the head, making two holes with the end of a paintbrush ready for the ears.

38 Make the ears as in step 28 and attach. Add a little pink nose too.

39 Roll out two teardrop shapes for the arms.

40 Paint in the facial details and dust the cheeks with a little petal dust.

41 Roll out two teardrop shapes, and a flattened ball.

42 Arrange them into a bow tie shape and attach to the neck.

43 Flatten a ball of paste, and pinch around the edges to make a bowl shape.

44 Twist two sausages of paste together to make a rope handle.

45 Attach the twist to the basket, securing at both sides with glue.

46 Roll some little egg shapes and arrange in the basket.

Materials

Modelling paste:
Purple
Blue
Green
Orange
Yellow
Red
White
Brown
White
Edible pen/paint: black
Edible glue
Lustre dust: pink

Tools

Craft knife / scalpel
Veining tool
Fine paintbrush
Large circle cutter
Toothpicks

1 Firstly let's make the clouds at the end of the rainbow!

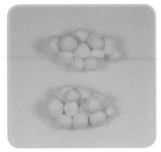

2 Roll out lots of differently sized white balls and arrange into a cloud shape.

3 Roll out some paste thinly and cover the balls to make a cloud. Define the bubbles with the soft end of the veining tool.

4 Make two clouds – one for each end of the rainbow.

5 Roll out thin sausages of paste in your chosen rainbow colours.

6 Start to arrange them one by one around a large circle cutter, adding a little edible glue in between each colour.

7 Once all your colours are in place, trim the ends so it will sit flush on your cake. Set aside to dry.

8 Now for some simple trees for your creatures to sit under!

9 Roll out a tapered sausage, and insert a toothpick through the centre.

10 Add a ball of green paste on top.

11 Add little flattened balls of paste for the blossom. You could add some small blossom shapes if you prefer.

12 Hey chicks!

13 Roll out a ball of paste, and taper it at one end. Flick the tapered end up with your finger.

14 Roll out a teardrop shape and flatten for the wing. Add a tiny teardrop shape for the beak.

15 Add little balls of paste for the head feathers.

16 Attach two small teardrop shapes for the tail feathers.

17 Paint or draw on the eyes, and brush the cheeks with a little petal dust.

18 Roll out a small yellow ball for the chick's body.

19 Add two small flattened teardrop shapes for the wings, turning them up slightly at the tips.

20 Add a little teardrop shape for the beak, and two further teardrop shapes for the feet.

21 Paint on some eyes, and brush the cheeks with a little petal dust.

22 Spring is the perfect time for little lambs to come out to play!

23 Roll out a teardrop shape for the lamb's body, insert a toothpick ready to take the head.

24 Roll out two teardrop shapes, and open the large end up. Insert a further teardrop shape in brown for the hooves.

25 Indent the hooves to add detail and attach the legs to the body.

26 Make the arms in the same way as the legs, but just slightly smaller and glue in place.

27 Add a large ball for the head.

28 Cut out an oval shape for the face and glue in place.

29 Make two teardrop shapes, and two smaller flesh coloured teardrop shapes and stick together.

30 Stick the ears to the side of the head.

31 Roll four tiny teardrop shapes and attach to the top of the head.

32 Paint or draw on the facial details and dust the cheeks with a little petal dust.

33 Lamby has a little bunny friend!

34 Roll a teardrop shape for the body, and attach two flattened teardrop shapes for the feet. Insert a toothpick through the body.

35 Attach two small teardrop shapes for the arms and two little feet, as shown.

36 Roll a large ball for the head, and with the end of a paintbrush make two holes on the top of the head ready for the ears.

37 Make two ears, as in Step 29, bend one over slightly and set aside to dry before placing them on the head.

38 Attach a contrasting colour to the face as shown.

39 Attach the ears with a little edible glue.

40 Add a little ball of pink for the nose, and paint on the facial details, adding blush with a little petal dust.

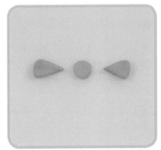

41 Roll out two teardrop shapes and little ball of paste to make the bow.

42 Attach the bow to the head.

43 Now let's make lots of pretty flowers for the rest of the cake.

44 Roll out 5 teardrop shapes, and indent each one down the centre with a veining tool. Arrange into a blossom shape.

45 Flatten a ball of paste and attach it to the centre of the blossom.

46 Make the leaf in the same way as the petals, and attach.

Easter Basket

Materials

Modelling paste:
Brown
Green
Yellow
Pale blue
White
Trex / Vegetable Shortening
Royal icing
Edible glue

Tools

Craft knife / scalpel
Foam modelling pad
Ball tool, Cone tool
Veining tool
24 gauge green floral wire
Needle nose pliers
Fondant extruder (optional)
Cutters: Hydrangea, blossom plunger, 6 petal blossom, daffodil, daisy plunger, ivy leaf plunger
Hydrangea mold
Flower formers
Piping bag, Piping tip #2
Sieve, Toothpicks

1 Roll and cover a cake board – large enough to fit your chosen cake/basket size – with green paste or fondant. Set aside to dry.

2 Roll (or extrude) a very long sausage of brown paste. Fold in half and twist together to create a rope effect basket handle.

3 Shape as a basket handle and insert a toothpick into each end. Set aside to dry.

4 You could either make the basket with a large sandwiched cake inside, or as a small topper using krispie treats.

5 Roll long sausages of brown fondant. Cut strips the height of the basket and attach one vertically. Next, cut horizontal strips.

6 Glue on in a basket weave pattern, placing vertical strips at the end of the alternating horizontal strips.

7 Twist another sausage of brown fondant together in the same manner as the basket handle. Top the basket with it.

8 Use a toothpick to poke holes where the handle will be placed. Attach the handle.

9 Flatten a large piece of white fondant in the center of the basket. Set aside.

10 An Easter basket needs flowers! First, let's make some cute and easy filler flowers!

11 Make small hooks in 4 ½ inch lengths of floral wire with a pair of needle nose pliers. You will need enough for all the different flowers you will make.

12 Roll out blue paste very thinly.

13 Cut out small blossoms.

14 Place blossom on the soft side of the modelling pad and thin the petals with a ball tool.

15 Dampen a hooked wire and just barely insert it into the center of the blossom. Stick each blossom into a cake dummy to dry.

16 Once dry, pipe royal icing centers. Allow to dry completely.

17 Now let's make hydrangea blossoms.

18 To make the centre, roll a tiny ball of white paste into a tear drop shape.

19 Dampen the wire hook with edible glue and insert it into the narrow end.

20 Pinch the bottom and remove the excess to make a small ball on the end of the wire.

21 Use a knife tool to mark the centre into four sections. Set aside in a cake dummy to dry.

22 When centres are dry, roll pink paste very thinly and cut out the hydrangea blossom.

23 Run your finger along the edge of the cutter to ensure a clean edge to the blossom.

24 Place the blossom in the center of the veining mold and press together firmly. Remove carefully.

25 Brush the centre with edible glue and insert the wired centre. Pinch gently. Place in a flower former or hang upside down to dry.

26 Now to make some sunny Easter daffodils!

27 Roll out yellow paste very thinly and cut out the daffodil blossom shape.

28 Place the blossom on the firm side of a foam pad. Vein the petals with the veining tool.

29 Place the blossom in a flower former while you make the trumpet.

30 To make the daffodil trumpet, roll a small amount of yellow paste over a medium hole in the modelling pad to make a 'Mexican hat'.

31 Place a six petal blossom cutter over the nub and cut out.

32 Use the cone tool to hollow out the centre.

33 Pinch the edges of the trumpet to thin them.

34 Dampen a hooked wire with edible glue and insert it through the centre of the trumpet.

35 Brush the center of the daffodil with edible glue and insert the wired trumpet. Allow to dry in a flower former.

36 Now let's make some cheerful daisies!

37 Roll out white paste very thinly and cut out daisy blossoms.

38 Use a ball tool to thin the petals. Place the blossom in a flower former.

39 To make the daisy center, roll a very small ball of yellow paste.

40 Dampen a hooked wire and insert it into the ball.

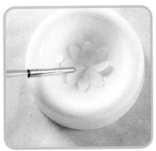

41 Brush the centre of the daisy blossom with edible glue. Insert the wired centre.

42 Press the daisy center against a wire mesh strainer or sieve to create texture. Place in a flower former to dry.

43 Roll out green paste very thinly and cut out ivy leaves.

44 Attach the ivy leaves randomly around the edge of the basket with edible glue.

45 Trim floral wires and arrange the flowers on your cake or topper.

46 Place the Easter basket in the centre of your cake board. Trim the edge of the board with pretty ribbon.

Easter Basket Cupcakes

Materials

Modelling paste:
Brown
Green
Yellow
Pale blue
White
White nonpareils
Edible glue

Tools

Craft knife / scalpel
Foam modelling pad
Ball tool
Pastry circle cutters
Blossom plunger cutter
Piping bag
Piping tip #3
Small bow mold
Toothpicks

1 Cut out one scalloped topper disc for each cupcake.

2 Use a piping tip #3 to cut out small holes in the scallops. Set aside to dry.

3 Use a small rolling pin to indent a ball of white paste. This will create the base for the floral nest.

4 Cut out lots of different coloured flowers with small blossom plunger cutter. Attach to the nest with edible glue.

5 Brush the center of each flower with some edible glue and drop one little white nonpareil into each flower.

6 Roll a small egg shape and place in centre of nest.

7 Roll then twist together two thin ropes of brown paste for the basket handle. Set aside to dry.

8 Shape a ball of brown paste so that the bottom is flat and the top is bulbous.

9 Flip the fondant over and flatten out the bottom with your fingers to create a 'brim'.

10 Use a small scalloped cutter to cut this brim, leaving a cute scalloped edge.

11 Indent the scallops with a small ball tool. Flip the basket over.

12 Add a ball of white paste to the top, before making and adding lots of blossoms as before.

13 Mould or make (see p. 15) two light blue bows per Easter basket.

14 Attach the basket handle and finish it off with the blue bows.

Materials

Modelling paste:
Yellow, Orange
Green, Purple
Pink, Blue
Brown, White
Black
Food colour: green,
yellow
Petal dust: pink
Edible glue

Tools

Craft knife / scalpel
Circle cutters
½" heart cutter
½" tear drop cutter
Blossom cutters
Fine paint brush
Tulle (optional)

1 If you are placing your chicks on a board, first cover this in blue fondant or paste.

2 Use green and yellow food colour to paint a grass effect onto the board, as shown.

3 For the chicks, roll some yellow paste into an egg shape and flatten the bottom.

4 Roll a piece of brown paste into a log shape, scoring to add a wood texture. Add a little heart shaped 'carving'.

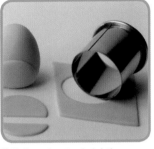

5 Roll and cut a brightly coloured paste circle, trim as shown and glue to the bottom of the boy chick's body.

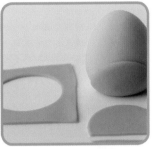

6 Do the same with pink or purple for the body of the girl chick.

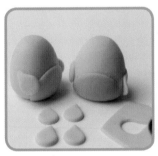

7 Roll and cut two yellow teardrop shapes for the wings. Glue to the sides of each body.

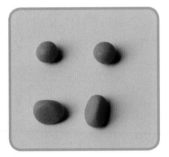

8 Roll two little orange cone shapes for the beaks and glue in place.

9 Either use a tiny piping nozzle to cut small black dots for eyes, or drawn or paint them on.

10 To make a tiny hat, cut a small tulle square and attach it to head with a little ball for the bonnet on top.

11 Roll out various colours of paste. Cut out little blossoms, and roll up strips of paste to form small roses.

12 Roll out green paste and use a small tear drop cutter to form leaves. Pinch together the rounded ends.

13 Place the log on the blue circle, or directly onto cake. Glue the leaves and flowers around the log's base.

14 Attach the chicks onto the log. Blush their cheeks using pink petal dust.

Cute Easter Cupcakes

HAPPY EASTER

Materials

Modelling paste:
Yellow, Orange
Green, Purple
Pink, Blue
Brown, White
Grey, Black
Food colouring: black,
white
Petal dust: pink
Edible glue

Tools

Craft knife / scalpel
Veining tool
Quilting tool
Circle cutters
Cutters: oval, teardrop,
leaf
Blossom cutters
Fine paint brush
Toothpicks

1 Cut cupcake topper discs from green paste. Stipple a grass effect with a grass piping tip or bunch of toothpicks.

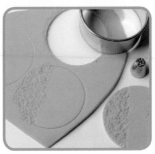

2 Stipple some other discs on only one side of the circle...the 'dirt' will cover the plain part.

3 You should make one topper disc for each cupcake you have baked!

4 Roll grey paste and either use a veining tool or a textured roller to add a 'cobbled' effect. Trim to make a little path shape.

5 Roll some brown paste and cut a third away, then texture a 'dirt' effect with a toothpick.

6 Do the same to make a larger 'dirt' section for some toppers.

7 Add these 'path' and 'dirt' sections to the green topper discs.

8 Roll and cut some green strips and cut into them to create a grass effect.

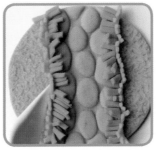

9 Glue the base of these pieces on either side of the path piece. We will add flowers later.

10 Roll a yellow body and head for the chick. Insert a toothpick, and add stitched detail with quilting tool.

11 Repeat the same steps to make a white body and head for bunny, again inserting a toothpick to support the head.

12 For the chick's feet and legs, roll an orange bulb shape and flatten and shape the feet as shown.

13 Roll an oval for the body area, trim the top part away and glue to each body as shown.

14 For the 'dirt' the bunny is sitting on, cut a smaller scalloped piece in brown, texture and add to topper disc.

15 Glue the body to the circle, then roll and pinch two pieces of white to form legs and paws. Indent with veining tool.

16 Make little carrots from cones of orange paste, and cut tiny leaf shapes. Glue in place in front of bunny.

17 Now roll and pinch two white arms and add paw details with veining tool. Glue to sides of body.

18 Use a tiny piping tip to cut black dots for eyes and a larger one for pink cheeks and nose. Paint or draw on eye details.

19 Cut two oval shapes in white for ears, and smaller ovals in pink. Layer as shown and glue ears to head.

20 Roll tiny Easter eggs in a mix of colours and add to topper. Paint white dots on bunny's ears and eggs.

21 Now add the chick's body to a green topper disc. Add some eggs around his body.

22 Roll some yellow paste and cut out two teardrop shapes for wings. Mark with veining tool and glue to sides.

23 Roll a tiny orange ball and pinch for the nose, then add two small teardrops below nose.

24 Add two more teardrops to top of head. Cut or paint on tiny black eyes. Add eyelashes and blush to face.

25 Attach head to body. Add white dots to eyes. Decorate eggs with white dots and add little blossoms.

26 Make a cute little shovel from a brown paste sausage and flat, grey piece of paste.

27 Take a topper disc that has a brown 'dirt' section, add a small 'dirt' area where the spade is 'digging' and little eggs.

28 Paint white dots and decorations on eggs. Add some flowers.

29 Cut lots of little blossoms and add to the 'dirt' section of a topper as shown.

30 Also add some flowers onto the grass toppers you made earlier.

31 To make a basket shape roll or cut a thick brown oval for the base.

32 Roll, cut and texture a long strip for the basket sides. Roll small sausages for handles and attach to sides.

33 Secure basket on topper disc. Roll white ball and two smaller ones for bunny head and paws. Indent paws and glue in place.

34 Make two small ears as shown. Poke holes in head and glue ears in place.

35 Glue carrots and eggs behind the bunny's head and on the topper.

36 Paint white dots onto the eggs.

37 For the egg basket start with a thick round base.

38 Roll, cut and texture a long strip for the basket sides. Glue around base.

39 Roll and cut one long strip and two shorter, angled strips to add a ribbon detail around the basket.

40 Finish the ribbon bow using two strips of paste, as shown.

41 Glue some eggs on the basket and around the circle. Decorate eggs with white dots.

42 Roll a brown ball and add texture with toothpicks. Insert a toothpick down the center and glue to disc.

43 Roll out a brown rectangle and paint on wording.

44 Slide the sign down onto the toothpick and glue some eggs on the circle.

45 Glue three carrots and an egg to the sign's base.

46 Finish by adding details to the eggs and flowers.

Materials

Modelling paste:
Light yellow
Light orange
Light green
Purple, Baby Blue
Soft Pink
Cream
Black
White
Petal dust: pink
Edible pen: black
Edible glue

Tools

Craft knife / scalpel
Ball tool
Veining tool
Cutters: round, oval, heart
Paint brush
Toothpicks

1 Roll a smooth ball for each bunny head.

2 Roll an oval shape for each body and insert a toothpick ready to support the head. Allow body to dry before adding head.

3 Roll and cut a thin oval of white and glue to each bunny face as shown.

4 Dot on eyes with edible black pen, or cut tiny paste eyes using a small piping tip as shown. Add a pink nose to each bunny too.

5 Roll four white ovals for the ears and use your ball tool to indent the centers of the ears. Bend the tips over slightly.

6 Roll and cut pink ovals to fit inside the white ears. Glue ears onto heads, using spaghetti to support if needed.

7 Roll small teardrop shapes for the arms and feet, gluing in place.

8 Make a tiny top hat from a cylinder and a flat circle of black paste. Glue together and add to boy bunny's head, using spaghetti as a support.

9 Cut and glue two small hearts together, plus a tiny circle to form a bow. Glue in place on boy bunny.

10 Roll and cut a thin square of cream paste for the veil. Glue behind one ear of girl bunny.

11 Roll lots of coloured Easter eggs, then roll small roses from strips of paste too.

12 Glue lots of little roses on the girl bunny to form a bouquet and around her veil.

13 If placing the bunnies on a disc, cut a thick white paste disc. Glue the eggs and the roses as shown.

14 Glue the bunnies to the base. Blush the cheeks and add shading under ears, arms and leg seams with pink petal dust.

Materials

Modelling paste:
Light Yellow
Daffodil yellow
Baby blue, Orange
Light green, Purple
Pink, Black, White
Food colouring: brown,
white
Petal dust: pink, yellow
Edible glue

Tools

Craft knife / scalpel
Veining tool
Ball tool
Pastry cutters
Blossom cutter
6 petal flower cutter
Small teardrop cutters
Foam pad
Small paintbrush

1 For each cupcake, cut a larger fluted disc and a smaller plain one, layering baby blue and lemon discs.

2 For the chicks, cut a small circle for head, slightly smaller for body and trim as shown. Add two small teardrops for wings.

3 Roll and cut some green teardrops and texture for grass. Add little blossom flowers on top.

4 Roll some tiny Easter eggs, and add in between wings and on the topper disc.

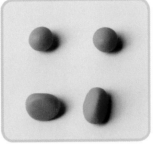

5 Roll and pinch a tiny orange cone for the nose. Glue it to the centre of chick's head.

6 Draw on eyes or cut tiny black dots using piping tip. Add blush to the cheeks, paint on hair and white dots to eggs.

7 For each daffodil, roll and cut out a 6 petal flower. Place flower on foam and indent each petal with the ball tool.

8 Form the trumpet from a yellow paste oval. Hollow out with ball tool, then add details and texture with veining tool.

9 Roll, cut and texture some white paste strips to look like wooden fence pieces. Glue to topper disc as shown.

10 Cut some small green leaves with teardrop cutter. Glue them on the circles with daffodil on top.

11 Roll 3 little Easter eggs for each topper. Paint on white dots and glue in place.

12 Cut more little leaves to go alongside some small blossom flowers.

13 Cut lots of little blossom flowers and glue them on top of the leaves.

14 Dust the trumpet of the daffodil with yellow petal dust.

Easy Easter Cupcakes

Materials

Modelling paste:
Pink
Yellow
Orange
Green
Lilac
White
Edible paint: black, white
Petal dust: pink

Tools

Craft knife / scalpel
Veining tool
Round pastry cutters
Small heart cutter
Toothpicks

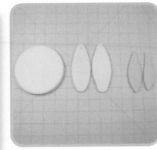

1 Roll and cut a white paste circle for the bunny head and two ovals for ears. Cut two smaller pink inner ears.

2 Assemble all parts on a slightly larger cupcake topper disc. Fold down one ear and allow to dry.

3 Add a tiny pink heart nose and paint/draw on the eye and mouth details. Dust cheeks with pink petal dust.

4 Cut the flat bunny shape from a small circle for head and crop a larger circle for the body. Make ears as before.

5 Add facial details, and a small ball, textured with toothpicks, for the tail. See Step 7 for the bow tie, painting on white dots.

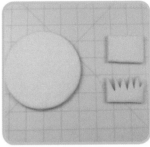

6 Cut a circle of yellow paste for the chick's head, and cut spikes from a small rectangle for the feathers.

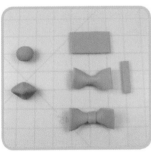

7 Pinch tiny ball of paste to make beak. And make a small bow as shown.

8 Assemble all parts on a cupcake topper disc and add facial details, as before.

9 Cut your chick body using one smaller circle for head and one circle the same size as topper disc, cropped.

10 Add texture to wings with veining tool and twist a little paste into a cute curl. Add facial details.

11 Cut a carrot shape as shown. Cut a rectangle of green paste with your scalpel to form spikes.

12 Mount on a contrasting cupcake topper disc and texturize carrot using the veining tool.

13 Cut a cute egg shape and mount on a contrasting cupcake topper disc.

14 Create simple decorations using paste strips, dots and zig zags!

Materials

Modelling paste:
Yellow
Orange
White
Edible paint: black
Petal dust: pink

Tools

Craft knife / scalpel
Veining tool
Round pastry cutters
Foam cupcake dome formers
Small heart cutter
Star cutters
Small paintbrush
Toothpicks

1 Let's start with some cute little chick cupcakes!

2 For each chick, cut a circle of yellow paste, place to dry lightly over a cupcake dome former.

3 For the 'hatching' chick, cut a separate circle of white paste, then cut in half.

4 Use a knife or scalpel tool to cut out shards of paste. Attach to the top and bottom of a yellow dome.

5 Add eyes, a beak (pinch a small ball of orange paste) and dust cheeks with pink petal dust.

6 For the second design, cut two leaf shapes of yellow paste and use a veining tool to add 'feather' details.

7 Attach the wings either side then paint on the facial details as shown. Add a cute curl of yellow paste.

8 This chick is coming out feet first!

9 Cut a circle of white paste, then cut out two star shapes as shown, then add 'cracks' using a veining tool.

10 Add a thin layer of yellow paste behind the stars and dry over a dome former.

11 Roll and cut paste for each leg as shown. Add 'wrinkles' with veining tool. Attach to dome, trimming to fit.

12 This little chick has arrived in time for Easter!

13 Repeat Steps 9 and 10 but cut a single star only from the centre. Roll a body and head for the chick.

14 Attach a white star to the head, little wings and facial details. Assemble with glue on your cupcake topper.

Easter Bow Cake

Materials

Modelling paste:
Pink
Lilac
Mint green
Lemon
White
Edible paint: black
Petal dust: pink

Tools

Craft knife / scalpel
Veining tool
Quilting tool
Ribbon cutter
Egg shaped cutter

1 Begin with a simply covered cake (ours is an 8" round and 4" deep).

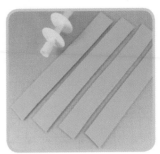

2 Start by creating the side 'ribbons' in the colour(s) of your choice. Use a ribbon cutter to make four strips, approx. 20cm x 2.5cm (8" x 1").

3 Add optional detail with your quilting tool.

4 Attach the four strips to the sides of your cake, as shown, trimming any overlap at the centre.

5 To create the loopy bow, create a further 16 ribbon strips (as Step 2) in your choice of colours.

6 Fold each ribbon over in the centre, gluing the ends together. Pinch into a fold at the join and glue.

7 Thread the loops over a rolling pin/cardboard tube and allow to dry until firm so they hold their shape.

8 Remove the loops from the roll and leave to dry on their sides. Support with rolled up kitchen paper, if necessary.

9 Take eight of the ribbon loops and attach to the cake, pinched ends in the middle, as shown.

10 Create your second layer with five more loops on top of the first layer, gluing in place, as shown.

11 Finally attach a single loop to the centre.

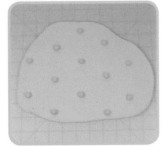

12 To create cute Easter egg motifs, roll some of your paste flat then dot around little contrasting paste balls.

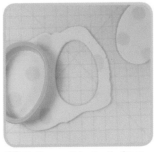

13 Roll over this gently from top to bottom then from side to side until the dots are flattened. Cut out your egg shapes.

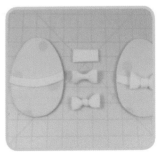

14 Add a strip of paste around the centre and a cute little bow, as shown. Glue to sides of cake.

Burrowing Bunny

Materials

Modelling paste:
White
Pink
Mint green
Orange
Black
Edible paint: black
Petal dust: pink
Rice krispie treats
Oreo/chocolate cookies

Tools

Craft knife / scalpel
Veining tool
Toothpicks

1 Start with a simply covered cake...we used green fondant to look like grass.

2 Mould rice krispie treats (RKT) into a head shape for your bunny character.

3 Cover this head with white paste and smooth into shape.

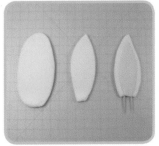

4 Cut two ears from thick white paste, plus pink inner ears. Glue together, inserting toothpicks for support. Set aside to dry.

5 Add two flattened balls of white paste, a little pink nose and mouth, plus two small black eyes. Draw on eyelashes.

6 Roll a ball of white paste, depress lightly at the back. Use a veining tool to create paw details.

7 For the feet, roll two flat ovals, adding a smaller pink oval. Shape toes using veining tool.

8 Add a few oreos or dark coloured cookies to a bag...

9 ...and crush with a rolling pin to create 'soil'.

10 Spread edible glue on top of the cake and press the crushed cookies into it to secure.

11 Attach the head and paws to the cake, inserting wooden skewers/toothpicks for support, if necessary.

12 Glue the feet to the front.

13 Create a carrot top from orange paste and three cones of green paste. Add detail with veining tool.

14 Create flat carrots and leaf shapes to decorate the sides of your cake. Score to add texture.

RECIPES ♥ TUTORIALS

Cake & Bake ACADEMY

Est. 2014

RESOURCES ♥ INSPIRATION

The Cute & Easy Cake Toppers Collection is a fantastic range of mini tutorial books covering a wide range of party themes!

Oh Baby!
Cute & Easy Cake Toppers for any Baby Shower, Christening, Birthday or Baby Celebration!

Princesses, Fairies & Ballerinas!
Cute & Easy Cake Toppers for any Princess Party or Girly Celebration!

Puppies and Kittens & Pets, Oh My!
Puppies, Kittens, Bunnies, Pets and more!

Tiny Tea Parties!
Mini Food and Tiny Tea Parties That Look Good Enough To Eat!

Passion for Fashion!
Cute & Easy Cake Toppers! Shoes, Bags, Make-up and more! Mini Fashions That Look good Enough To Eat!

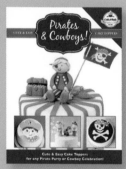

Pirates & Cowboys!
Cute & Easy Cake Toppers for any Pirate Party or Cowboy Celebration!

Cute and Easy Cake Toppers
Brenda Walton from Sugar High shows how to make cute and easy cake topper characters at home!

PLUS:
Cake Toppers for Boys!
Superheroes, Dinosaurs and more!
Cake Toppers for Girls!
Tons of girly cake topper cuteness!
Cake Toppers for Men!
Many manly mini cake toppers!
Farmyard Fun!
Tractors, Diggers and Farm Animals Galore!
Circus Time!
All The Fun Of The Big Top!
Jungle Fun!
Lions and Tigers and Monkeys, Oh My!
Xmas Time!
Cute & Easy Xmas Cake Toppers!
and more!

Available in Paperback or instant PDF!

All books are available on Paperback : £6.95 / $10.95
Also available on instant PDF for just £2.95 / $5.95 from: www.cakeandbakeacademy.com

Search on Amazon under 'Cake & Bake Academy' or visit:
www.cakeandbakeacademy.com

Printed in Great Britain
by Amazon